Preparing The
Learning Environment

Dr. Sarah Aiono
Linda Cheer

Preparing the Learning Environment

By Dr. Sarah Aiono and Linda Cheer

Published by Taonga Auaha Publishing
Napier, New Zealand

Copyright © 2024 by Sarah Aiono and Linda Cheer

All rights reserved. No part of this book may be reproduced, stored in a retrieval system, or transmitted in any form or by any means, electronic, mechanical, photocopying, recording, or otherwise, without the prior written permission of the publisher, except for the inclusion of brief quotations in a review.

ISBN: 978-0-473-71961-6

First Edition: August 2024

For information about permission to reproduce selections from this book, write to Taonga Auaha Publishing at the address below:

Taonga Auaha Publishing
64 Longview Road, Poraiti, RD2, Napier
Email: info@longwortheducation.co.nz
Website: www.longwortheducation.co.nz

Cover Design by: Saravanan Ponnaiyan (Cropmarks Prepress Services)

Printed in New Zealand

Disclaimer:

The authors and publisher have made every effort to ensure that the information in this book is accurate and up to date at the time of publication. However, the authors and publisher do not assume and hereby disclaim any liability to any party for any loss, damage, or disruption caused by errors or omissions whether such errors or omissions result from negligence, accident, or any other cause.

Acknowledgements

We wish to acknowledge all the educators and thought leaders who have inspired and supported us in the creation of this book. Your dedication and passion for education are truly appreciated.

Special thanks to St Patricks' School, Napier; Te Kura o Take Kārara, Wānaka; Te Whai Hiringa, Flaxmere Northcote Primary, Auckland; Allandale School, Whakatāne, Oxford Crescent School, Upper Hutt and Golden Sands School, Pāpāmoa, for their contributions of photos to this handbook. Your support has greatly enhanced the quality, inspiration and visual understanding of the power of play in our classrooms

We also wanted to share our appreciation for the experience and knowledge of Associate Professor Tara McLaughlin, Massey University, who has been a guide, mentor and support over the last decade. Her wisdom has been instrumental in putting this handbook series together.

Table of Contents

Introduction:	Embracing Play-Based Learning in Diverse Educational Contexts	1
Chapter 1:	Fostering Choice and Flexibility in Learning Environments	5
Chapter 2:	Enhancing Creativity with Small Loose Parts	17
Chapter 3:	Incorporating Large Loose Parts in Outdoor Play	25
Chapter 4:	Promoting Learning to the School Community	33
Conclusion:	Shaping the Future through Play-Based Learning	43
About the Authors		47

Te Whai Hiringa School

Introduction: Embracing Play-Based Learning in Diverse Educational Contexts

Welcome to this comprehensive guide, aimed at assisting educators in crafting effective learning environments that foster and leverage evidence-informed play pedagogy. This is the first of a series of handbooks attempting to bridge the gap for educators between policy, pedagogy and everyday classroom practices and decisions. Each serves not only as a practical tool but also as a source of inspiration for those dedicated to nurturing dynamic, inclusive, and stimulating educational settings.

Understanding Play-Based Learning

Play-based learning is a pedagogical approach that recognises the intrinsic value of play in children's development and learning processes. It transcends the traditional view of play as merely a leisure activity, presenting it instead as a vital medium through which children explore their environment, develop essential skills, and construct their understanding. This approach is grounded in the belief that children are active participants in their learning journey and that the environment plays a pivotal role in shaping these experiences.

Play-Based Learning for Children Aged 5-12 Years

The power of play-based learning is often associated with early childhood, but its benefits extend well into the middle childhood years (ages 5-12). For children in this age group, play continues to be a crucial element for learning and development.

Play-based learning adapts to the developmental stages of children, offering age-appropriate challenges and experiences that are both engaging and educational. By integrating play into the curriculum for older children, we provide them with a more holistic and enjoyable learning experience. Play-based learning for older children can take various forms, including experiential, hands-on learning, role-playing, child-led inquiry, and exploration-based learning. These activities offer rich opportunities for children to develop advanced cognitive skills, such as problem-solving, critical thinking, and creativity.

Benefits of Play-Based Learning

The benefits of play-based learning for children aged 5-12 years are multifaceted:

- **Cognitive Development:** Play stimulates brain development and aids in the acquisition of academic skills. It allows children to explore concepts in a real-world context, enhancing their understanding and retention.
- **Social and Emotional Growth:** Play provides opportunities for children to develop social skills, such as cooperation, negotiation, and conflict resolution. It also supports emotional development by allowing children to express their feelings and understand the perspectives of others.
- **Physical Development:** Physical play promotes motor skills, coordination, and overall physical health. It is essential for the physical well-being of growing children.
- **Creativity and Innovation:** Play-based learning encourages children to use their imagination and creativity, fostering innovative thinking and problem-solving abilities.

The Aim of This Handbook: The Learning Environment

This handbook delves into the **crucial foundation of play-based learning: the learning environment**. Understanding its design and impact is the first step for educators embarking on this pedagogical journey. We equip you with a unique **three-stage descriptor** – a roadmap to analyse, improve, and ultimately cultivate a vibrant space for playful learning. Whether you're starting with minimal play elements or actively refining your practices, this framework guides you through crucial stages:

Limited Implementation: This stage describes a learning environment that has minimal or basic elements of the chapter's focus. It identifies the characteristics of such settings, the impact on learning, and offers strategies for improvement. This stage is crucial for recognising the starting points and the potential areas for growth. Identify where you stand by recognizing basic play aspects and their learning outcomes. We help you strategize for growth from this essential starting point.

Developing Implementation: The second stage represents a transitional phase where the learning environment begins to incorporate more of the chapter's key elements. It outlines the characteristics of these evolving spaces, their impact on learning, and suggests strategies for further development. This stage is aimed at educators who are in the process of enhancing their learning environments. Witness your classroom evolve as you incorporate more playful elements. Understand how these changes impact learning and discover strategies for deeper development.

Strong Implementation: The final stage depicts an ideal learning environment that fully embraces the principles of the chapter. It describes the characteristics of such advanced settings, their positive impact on learning, and offers strategies for maintaining and evolving these environments. This stage serves as a goal or benchmark for educators to aspire to. Envision and strive for the ideal play-based classroom, bursting with rich opportunities for growth. Learn how to maintain and refine this advanced environment for maximum learning impact.

Each stage is accompanied by photos and real-life examples to provide visual representations and practical insights. This format not only helps educators assess their current learning environment and classroom practices, but also guides them through a progressive journey of improvement. By understanding and applying these stages, educators can create more effective, engaging, and supportive learning environments and align their classroom practices with the principles of play pedagogy.

Te Kura o Take Kārara

Conclusion

As educators, our mission is to create a learning experience that not only engage children intellectually but also nurture their overall development. Through this series of handbooks, we aim to shed light on the transformative power of play-based learning, encouraging educators to embrace this approach for children of all ages. By valuing and enhancing play in our educational practices, we empower our children to become curious, confident, and creative learners, laying the foundation for a lifelong journey of discovery and growth.

Fostering Choice and Flexibility in Learning Environments

Introduction: The Importance of Choice and Flexibility

Key Pedagogical Principles: Flexibility, Movement, Accessibility, Predictability

The learning environment is a canvas for children's exploration, creativity, and growth. In this chapter, we delve into the significance of offering a variety of learning spaces, examining how different setups impact children's play and learning experiences.

Choice as a Catalyst for Engagement and Ownership: Offering children choices in their learning environment is crucial for fostering their engagement and sense of ownership over their learning process. When children are given the opportunity to make choices, whether it's selecting activities, materials, or spaces, they feel more invested in their learning. This sense of ownership not only boosts their motivation but also encourages them to take responsibility for their learning journey. By making decisions, children learn to trust their instincts and develop confidence in their abilities, which is essential for their overall development.

Flexibility Encourages Exploration and Creativity: A flexible learning environment, one that adapts to the diverse needs and interests of children, is fundamental in nurturing exploration and creativity. Flexibility in the learning space means that children can manipulate their surroundings to suit their current interests or projects.

This adaptability allows for a variety of learning experiences, from quiet, focused activities to more dynamic, collaborative projects. Such an environment encourages children to think creatively, solve problems, and adapt to new situations, skills that are invaluable in their future academic and personal lives.

Benefits to Social and Emotional Development: Choice and flexibility in the learning environment also have significant benefits for children's social and emotional development. When children are allowed to make choices, they learn to negotiate, collaborate, and communicate their ideas and preferences with peers and educators. This fosters a sense of community and belonging, as children feel their voices are heard and valued. Moreover, the ability to choose and adapt their learning environment helps children develop coping strategies for managing their emotions and behaviours, leading to improved self-regulation skills.

Catering to Individual Learning Styles: Every child has a unique learning style, and a learning environment that offers choice and flexibility can cater to these individual differences. Some children might prefer quiet, secluded spaces for individual reflection, while others thrive in more dynamic, collaborative settings. By providing a variety of spaces and resources, educators can ensure that each child's learning needs and preferences are met. This personalised approach not only enhances learning outcomes but also helps in building a more inclusive and supportive educational setting.

Long-Term Academic Benefits: The impact of choice and flexibility in the learning environment extends beyond immediate engagement and creativity. Research has shown that such environments can lead to better academic outcomes in the long term. Children who are accustomed to making choices and adapting to different learning situations develop critical thinking and problem-solving skills. These skills are crucial for academic success and lifelong learning. Furthermore, the ability to adapt to various environments and collaborate with others prepares children for the diverse and ever-changing world they will face outside the classroom.

> Fostering choice and flexibility in learning environments is not just about creating a pleasant and engaging space for children. It's about equipping them with the skills, confidence, and adaptability they need to succeed in their educational journey and beyond. As educators, it is our responsibility to create these dynamic, inclusive, and responsive spaces that cater to the diverse needs of every child.

Preparing The Learning Environment

Three-Stage Practice Descriptions and Examples:

To provide a comprehensive understanding and practical guidance, we have incorporated a unique three-stage descriptor to unpack how choice and flexibility can be observed in learning environments. This descriptor serves as a tool to assess and enhance the learning environments based on the principles discussed previously. In addition, at the end of this chapter, we have included a brief self-assessment checklist that can be used to reflect on your own environment, and possible adjustments you can make in order to promote further choice and flexibility for your students.

Limited Space and Choices

In settings where resources are minimal, the learning environment is often confined to traditional desks and tables with limited floor space. Such arrangements can significantly restrict the scope of play-based learning.

Characteristics: The primary feature of this level is the lack of variety. The space is often rigidly structured, with students confined to their desks for most activities. Large-scale play activities are not feasible due to space constraints.

Impact on Learning: This setup can limit children's ability to engage in diverse learning activities. It restricts their physical movement and curtails opportunities for imaginative and collaborative play.

Improvement Strategies: Even in constrained spaces, small changes can make a difference. Introducing movable furniture or creating a small corner for different activities can begin to open up opportunities for varied play.

Oxford Crescent School

Northcote Primary School

Fostering Choice and Flexibility in Learning Environments

Expanding Choices

As we move to a developing stage, classrooms begin to embrace diversity in learning spaces. These environments offer more than just desks; they include specific areas designated for varied activities.

Characteristics: This level sees the inclusion of floor areas for activities like construction play or imaginative scenarios. There might be limitations on outdoor play due to space or supervision challenges.

Impact on Learning: The introduction of designated play areas supports the development of specific skills and fosters a sense of autonomy among students. While outdoor play may be limited, the indoor diversity begins to cater to different learning and play styles.

Improvement Strategies: Maximising the use of available outdoor space and creatively using indoor areas can further enhance the learning environment. Simple additions like rugs for floor activities or portable play materials can make a significant difference.

Oxford Crescent School

A World of Choices

At the strong level, learning spaces transform into dynamic environments where students are immersed in a world of choices, both indoors and outdoors.

Characteristics: Here, tables and desks are versatile, supporting various activities. A significant portion of the classroom is dedicated to floor-based play. Outdoor areas are not just open spaces but are equipped with elements like water play areas and natural exploration zones.

Impact on Learning: This level of variety encourages students to take charge of their learning through play. It facilitates holistic development, catering to physical, cognitive, and social-emotional growth.

Improvement Strategies: Continuously evolving the space based on student interests and feedback can lead to even more effective learning environments. Engaging students in the design process can foster a deeper connection with their learning space.

Conclusion

It's imperative to reflect on the profound impact that choice and flexibility have in shaping the learning environments for children. The above has underscored the importance of creating spaces that not only accommodate but also celebrate the diverse needs and preferences of each child. Through the lens of our three-stage practice descriptions, we have seen how environments can evolve from limited to dynamic spaces, each stage offering unique opportunities and challenges.

The journey from limited spaces, characterised by a lack of variety and rigid structures, to a world of choices, where learning environments are rich with diverse and adaptable spaces, illustrates a transformative path in educational settings. This transformation is not merely about physical space rearrangement; it's about a paradigm shift in how we perceive and value the role of the environment in children's learning and development.

In settings with limited space and choices, we've seen how even small modifications can significantly enhance the learning experience, proving that resource constraints need not be a barrier to creating engaging and effective learning environments. As we move to developing stages, the introduction of diverse indoor and outdoor play areas begins to shape a more holistic approach to learning, catering to different styles and preferences.

At the strong implementation level, where students are immersed in a world of choices, the learning environment becomes a dynamic and interactive space that fosters holistic development. This level exemplifies the ideal scenario where flexibility and choice are embedded in every aspect of the learning environment, promoting cognitive, physical, and socio-emotional growth.

With creativity, thoughtful planning, and a commitment to continuous improvement, learning environments can be transformed to cater to a wide range of learning and play needs. The goal is not just to create pleasant spaces but to construct environments that are conducive to learning, exploration, and growth, regardless of the starting point.

> As educators and facilitators, our role extends beyond teaching; it involves creating and nurturing spaces that inspire, challenge, and support every child in their unique learning journey. By embracing the principles of choice and flexibility, we can create learning environments that are not only effective but also inclusive, dynamic, and responsive to the ever-changing needs of our students.

Northcote Primary School

Preparing The Learning Environment

Chapter 1 – Checklist 1:

Inside Learning Space

- How many different learning spaces have you created in your classroom?
- Are the learning spaces attractive and welcoming?
- Have you created a quiet space to cater for children who prefer a less noisy environment?
- Have you found ways to separate learning areas?
- Have you minimised the number of tables/ desks and chairs to create more floor space?
- Is the print material for your children displayed at their eye level?
- Have you set aside a space for teacher only resources?
- Have you arranged easy access to the outdoor area?

Outside Learning Space

- Does the outside area have a clearly defined boundary?
- Have you identified any hazards? How will you manage these, to ensure children have continued access to learning outside?
- Have you arranged the outside resources into attractive invitational settings?
- Have you ensured your children have access to water and sand?

Resource Accessibility and Management in Learning Environments

As we continue to explore the dynamics of play-based learning environments, it's crucial to address the organisation of these spaces, particularly in terms of resource accessibility and management. This aspect is fundamental in nurturing children's independence and responsibility within their learning journey.

Limited Organisation and Accessibility

In settings with minimal organisation, children often encounter obstacles in accessing and managing resources independently.

Characteristics: The main challenge at this level is the lack of organisation. Resources are not readily accessible to students, often necessitating adult intervention for access and management.

Impact on Learning: Such an environment can impede the development of children's independence and responsibility. It may also restrict their engagement and exploration in play-based activities.

Improvement Strategies: To improve organisation, consider introducing child-level storage and clear labelling. Encourage children to participate in tidying and organising to cultivate a sense of ownership.

St Patricks' School, Napier

Progressing Towards Self-Sufficiency

As we advance to a developing stage, classrooms demonstrate better organisation, with resources becoming more accessible to children without constant adult supervision.

Characteristics: Specific areas are designated for certain resources. Children can access some materials independently, though they often need reminders to return items after use.

Preparing The Learning Environment

Impact on Learning: This level of organisation starts to support children's autonomy and decision-making. It also fosters the development of responsibility as students learn to manage resources.

Improvement Strategies: Enhance visual cues for storage areas and consistently involve students in the organisation process to further develop their self-management skills.

Te Kura o Take Kārara

A Model of Self-Sufficiency and Order

In a highly organised learning environment, children independently access and manage a wide array of resources.

Characteristics: The classroom is thoughtfully arranged with clearly defined areas for different resources. Students can access most materials independently and are adept at returning items with minimal teacher intervention. Outdoor resources are also well managed.

Impact on Learning: This level of organisation empowers students to take charge of their learning environment. It promotes a sense of responsibility and enhances their ability to self-direct their learning and play.

Improvement Strategies: Continuously adapt the space based on student feedback and evolving needs to maintain a high level of organisation and independence.

Allandale School

Conclusion

A well-organised learning space is not just a backdrop for educational activities; it is a critical component in the fabric of a play-based environment. Such an environment does more than just facilitate ease of access to resources; it actively shapes the educational experience and developmental trajectory of children.

Facilitating Access and Fostering Independence: Easy access to resources in a well-organised learning space empowers children to take initiative. When children can independently reach for materials and tools, they develop a sense of autonomy. This autonomy is the bedrock of self-directed learning, where children begin to make choices about their learning activities, fostering a deeper engagement with the learning process.

Nurturing Responsibility and Self-Management: In an environment where children are involved in the organisation and maintenance of their space, they learn valuable lessons in responsibility. They understand the importance of taking care of their resources and the shared space. This involvement cultivates a sense of ownership, which in turn encourages them to act responsibly. Learning to return items after use, keeping the space tidy, and respecting shared materials are all aspects of self-management that are crucial for their future both in and out of educational settings.

Promoting Essential Life Skills: The skills developed in a well-organised learning environment extend far beyond the classroom walls. Independence, responsibility, and self-management are life skills that children will carry into adulthood. These skills are essential in various aspects of life, including personal relationships, future workplaces, and community involvement. By mastering these skills early on, children are better prepared for the challenges and opportunities they will encounter later in life.

Intentional Design and Student Involvement: The creation of such an environment requires intentional design. This means not only arranging physical spaces and resources in an accessible and logical manner but also considering the diverse needs and preferences of the children. Involving students in this process is crucial. When children contribute to the design and organisation of their learning space, they feel valued and heard. This involvement can increase their engagement with the learning process and deepen their connection to the educational environment.

Establishing a Conducive and Self-Sustaining Environment: Ultimately, the goal is to establish a learning environment that is both conducive to education and self-sustaining in its organisation. A well-organised space that is maintained through the collective efforts of students and educators can adapt and evolve over time, continually meeting the changing needs of its users. This dynamic and responsive environment ensures that the learning space remains relevant, effective, and supportive of the holistic development of every child.

In conclusion, the organisation of a learning space in a play-based environment is a critical factor that significantly influences the educational and developmental outcomes for children. By prioritising well-organised spaces and involving students in the process, educators can create a dynamic, engaging, and nurturing environment that equips children with essential life skills and prepares them for a successful future.

St Patricks' School, Napier

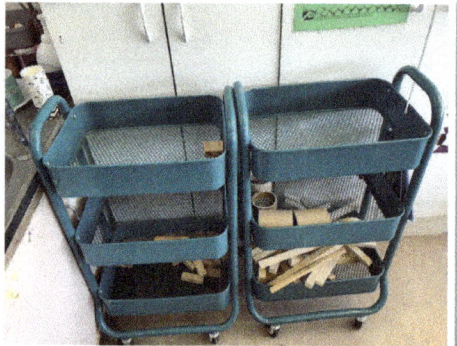
Allandale School

Chapter 1 – Checklist 2:

Are the available resources able to be seen and retrieved easily?

- Is there a space for teacher only resources?
- Is there an understanding that some loose parts be kept in specific places whilst others can be jumbled up?
- Is there a management system in place for pack up time?
- Is there an understanding of what is meant by consumables and where they are kept?
- Is there a specific place for projects that have not been finished?
- Is there an understanding that loose parts cannot be taken home but activities can be photographed?
- Is there an understanding about which resources can be taken outside and which need to remain in the classroom?

Enhancing Creativity with Small Loose Parts

Introduction

Key Pedagogical Principles: Child-Centred Learning, Creativity and Innovation, Holistic Development

This chapter delves deeply into the significance of small loose parts in enriching play-based learning environments, a facet of early childhood education that is often undervalued yet holds immense potential for fostering creativity and cognitive development. We explore how the diversity and accessibility of these resources can support creative and varied play experiences for children, underpinning a multitude of learning opportunities.

Small loose parts, which can include a wide array of items such as buttons, beads, pebbles, sticks, fabric scraps, and more, are fundamental in creating an environment that encourages children to explore, imagine, and invent. These materials are unique in their lack of specific instructions, allowing children the freedom to use them in limitless ways. This open-ended nature of small loose parts is what makes them so valuable in a play-based learning setting.

Why Small Loose Parts?

Fostering Creativity and Imagination: Small loose parts serve as tools for imagination. Unlike fixed toys or games with predetermined outcomes, these materials allow children to create their own narratives and structures. This freedom not only sparks creativity but also encourages children to think critically and innovatively.

Enhancing Fine Motor Skills and Coordination: Handling small items requires dexterity and precision, aiding in the development of fine motor skills. As children manipulate these parts, they improve their hand-eye coordination and develop skills crucial for writing, drawing, and other detailed activities.

Promoting Cognitive Development: The use of small loose parts in play can enhance cognitive abilities such as problem-solving, planning, and spatial awareness. Children learn to classify, sort, and sequence these items, which are foundational skills in mathematics and science.

Encouraging Language and Social Skills: When children play with loose parts together, they communicate and collaborate, sharing ideas and negotiating roles. This interaction is vital for language development and social skill acquisition, as children learn to express themselves and understand others.

Supporting Emotional Development: Play with small loose parts can be both a solitary and a shared experience, allowing children to express emotions and process experiences. It offers a safe space for children to explore feelings and ideas, contributing to emotional maturity.

Cultivating a Connection with the Natural World: Many small loose parts are natural materials, which helps children develop an appreciation and understanding of the environment. This connection fosters a sense of responsibility towards nature and an understanding of the world around them.

The incorporation of small loose parts in play-based learning environments is not just an addition of materials; it's a strategic approach to enhance the developmental aspects of play. By providing these resources, educators and caregivers offer a canvas for children to paint their ideas, learn new skills, and grow in a holistic manner. This chapter aims to highlight the myriad ways in which small loose parts

Preparing The Learning Environment

can be integrated into educational settings to maximise their potential in supporting children's learning and development.

In this chapter, we apply our structured three-stage practice descriptor to the world of small loose parts in play-based learning environments. This framework will guide us through the varying levels of incorporating small loose parts, from basic beginnings to rich, diverse applications. Each stage is designed to provide educators with a clear understanding of how small loose parts can be effectively used to enhance creativity and learning. To assist in the practical application of these concepts, the chapter concludes with a self-assessment checklist. This tool is aimed at helping educators evaluate their current use of small loose parts and identify opportunities for further integration and enhancement in their learning environments.

Limited Resource Variety

In environments where resource variety is limited, the availability of small loose parts is minimal, often confined to conventional educational materials.

Characteristics: The predominant feature at this level is a scarcity of creative play resources. The available items are typically curriculum-focused, such as maths equipment or reading games, providing limited opportunities for imaginative play.

Impact on Learning: This constrained range of resources limits children's ability to explore and create freely, potentially stifling their creativity and exploration.

Improvement Strategies: Introducing a range of easily accessible, non-prescriptive resources can begin to expand the scope of play. Simple items like recyclable materials or fabric scraps can significantly enhance creative opportunities.

Northcote Primary School

Northcote Primary School

Enhancing Creativity with Small Loose Parts

Growing Resource Diversity

Moving to a developing stage, classrooms start to incorporate a more diverse collection of small loose parts, encouraging varied types of play.

Characteristics: This stage introduces resources such as blocks, Lego, and natural materials. There is an increase in play options, though resources like dough and clay may still be utilised with structured tools.

Impact on Learning: The expanded variety of resources begins to nurture creativity and problem-solving skills. Children have more opportunities to experiment and engage in role-playing activities.

Improvement Strategies: Expanding the range of resources and encouraging their flexible use can further foster creativity. Providing open-ended materials like fabric pieces or natural elements can enhance imaginative play.

Allandale School

Longworth Forest School

A Rich Tapestry of Creative Materials

In a strong setting, the classroom becomes a treasure trove of small loose parts, offering a vast array of materials for creative exploration.

Characteristics: A broad spectrum of real and natural items is available, including unconventional resources like glass beads, feathers, and stones. These resources are accessible for a multitude of uses, both inside and outside the classroom.

Preparing The Learning Environment

Impact on Learning: This rich resource environment supports a high level of creative expression and innovation. Children can engage in complex play scenarios, building on their cognitive and social-emotional skills.

Improvement Strategies: Continuously updating and rotating resources based on children's interests and developmental stages can keep the environment stimulating and responsive to their evolving needs.

St Patrick's School, Napier

St Patrick's School, Napier

Conclusion

The availability and diversity of small loose parts play a pivotal role in cultivating a play-based learning environment that champions creativity, exploration, and cognitive development. This chapter has highlighted that through the thoughtful selection and presentation of a diverse range of materials, educators can significantly enhance the depth and breadth of children's play experiences and learning outcomes.

> Small loose parts, by their very nature, invite children to think outside the box, fostering an environment where imagination and innovation can flourish. These materials encourage children to create, dismantle, and re-imagine, leading to a deeper understanding of their world and the development of critical thinking skills. The use of such resources also supports the development of fine motor skills, as children manipulate small items in various ways.

Moreover, the inclusion of small loose parts in play-based learning settings promotes social and emotional development. As children engage in shared play scenarios, they learn to negotiate, collaborate, and express their ideas and feelings. This collaborative play nurtures empathy and understanding, essential components of social-emotional learning.

In conclusion, by integrating a rich array of small loose parts into the learning environment, educators can provide a dynamic and stimulating space that not only supports academic learning but also fosters the holistic development of children. Such environments prepare children not just for academic success but for life, equipping them with the creativity, problem-solving skills, and social competencies needed in an ever-changing world.

Northcote Primary School

Te Kura o Take Kārara

Chapter 2 - Checklist 1:

- Are you making use of school equipment as everyday resources to be used during play?
- Are the loose parts you have sourced open ended?
- Do you have a variety of natural resources e.g., shells, sticks, stones etc readily available?
- Do you have resources that could be designated junk or recyclable items?
- Have you limited the number of ready-made toys to be used during play?
- Have you limited the number of plastic resources?
- Have you ensured the loose parts meet the needs of your students?
- Do you have a plan for re energising the learning space with fresh loose parts?

St Patricks' School, Napier

Incorporating Large Loose Parts in Outdoor Play

Introduction

Key Pedagogical Principles: Experiential Learning, Outdoor Learning, Creativity and Innovation

Building on the foundational concepts introduced with small loose parts, let's shift focus to the transformative role of large loose parts in outdoor play environments. Large loose parts, encompassing a diverse range of bigger items such as wooden planks, tyres, large boxes, ropes, and natural elements like logs and stones, offer unique and dynamic opportunities for learning and development in school environments.

Why Large Junk at School?

Enhancing Physical Development: Large loose parts naturally encourage physical activity. As children lift, carry, and manipulate these items, they engage in a form of physical exercise that is crucial for their health and development. This type of play aids in developing gross motor skills, balance, and coordination, which are essential for overall physical well-being.

Promoting Collaborative Learning: The size and nature of large loose parts often necessitate teamwork. Children learn to collaborate, share ideas, and work together to achieve common goals, such as building a structure or creating a play scenario. This collaborative effort is vital for developing social skills and learning how to work effectively in groups.

Fostering Creativity and Problem-Solving: Large loose parts provide a canvas for imagination on a grander scale. Children are challenged to think creatively as they construct and interact with these materials. This type of play not only stimulates creativity but also enhances problem-solving skills, as children figure out how to balance, join, and use the materials in innovative ways.

Connecting with Nature: Especially when large loose parts include natural elements, they help children develop a connection with the natural world. Interacting with materials like wood, stones, and sand encourages an appreciation for nature and an understanding of the environment.

Creating Inclusive Play Opportunities: Large loose parts are versatile and can be used in a variety of ways, making them accessible and engaging for children with different interests and abilities. This inclusivity ensures that all children can participate and benefit from the play experiences these materials offer.

Enhancing the School Environment: The introduction of large loose parts transforms the outdoor space of a school into a more engaging and stimulating environment. This change can have a positive impact on the overall atmosphere of the school, making it a more inviting and exciting place for children to learn and grow.

Preparing The Learning Environment

As we explore the use of large loose parts in outdoor play environments, we continue to utilise our three-stage practice descriptor framework. This approach segments the integration of large loose parts into distinct stages, each representing a step forward in creating dynamic and engaging outdoor learning spaces. The stages range from initial incorporation to fully developed and varied environments. At the end of this chapter, educators will find a self-assessment checklist tailored to the use of large loose parts. This checklist serves as a reflective tool, enabling educators to assess their current outdoor environments and to plan strategic enhancements that further enrich children's play and learning experiences.

Minimal Outdoor Resources

At the minimal level, outdoor play environments are often devoid of large loose parts, which limits the scope of outdoor play and exploration.

Characteristics: The primary feature at this stage is the absence of large, interactive play items in the outdoor space. Students may have access to the outdoors but without the enrichment of additional resources like sand or water play areas.

Impact on Learning: The lack of diverse and engaging materials outdoors can restrict physical and creative development. Opportunities for imaginative and large-scale construction play are limited.

Improvement Strategies: Introducing basic large loose parts, such as cardboard boxes or simple construction materials, can begin to transform the outdoor space into a more dynamic play environment.

St Patricks' School, Napier

St Patricks' School, Napier

Incorporating Large Loose Parts in Outdoor Play

Growing Range of Outdoor Resources

As we move to a developing stage, the outdoor play area starts to feature a broader array of large loose parts.

Characteristics: There is a modest selection of large loose parts, like cardboard boxes and basic PE equipment. Access to elements like a water tray or a sand area is occasionally available, providing more diverse play opportunities.

Impact on Learning: The inclusion of these resources begins to encourage more complex play activities, fostering physical skills and cooperative play.

Improvement Strategies: Expanding the variety and complexity of outdoor loose parts, such as adding more challenging construction materials or natural elements, can further enhance outdoor play experiences.

Te Kura o Take Kārara

Longworth Forest School

Incorporating Large Loose Parts in Outdoor Play

Preparing The Learning Environment

A Rich and Varied Outdoor Play Environment

At the strong level, the outdoor play area is a rich and diverse environment, filled with a wide range of large loose parts.

Characteristics: Students have access to an extensive variety of materials, including construction elements like wood planks, pipes, and ropes. These resources are complemented by sensory play areas with water, sand, and mud. The space allows for a wide range of play types, from physical activities to imaginative construction.

Impact on Learning: This environment supports comprehensive development, including fine and gross motor skills, problem-solving, creativity, and social interaction.

Improvement Strategies: Continuously evolving the outdoor space based on student feedback and introducing new challenges can keep the environment stimulating and engaging.

Longworth Forest School

Longworth Forest School

Conclusion

The incorporation of large loose parts in outdoor play environments is instrumental in creating rich, engaging, and developmentally appropriate play experiences. Just as small loose parts enhance indoor play, large loose parts transform outdoor spaces into arenas of limitless imagination and physical activity. These materials encourage children to engage in a broader spectrum of play, from constructing large-scale structures to engaging in sensory exploration with elements like sand and water.

> Large loose parts in outdoor settings offer unique opportunities for physical development, including gross motor skills and coordination. As children lift, move, and manipulate these larger items, they develop strength and physical confidence. Additionally, these resources foster teamwork and social interaction, as children often work together to build and create, learning valuable lessons in cooperation and communication.

Moreover, the variety and scale of large loose parts challenge children to think creatively and solve problems in innovative ways. They learn to envision and execute complex projects, enhancing their cognitive abilities and fostering a sense of achievement and self-efficacy.

By thoughtfully selecting and arranging outdoor materials, educators can significantly enhance the quality and depth of children's outdoor play. This approach not only supports a broad range of learning opportunities but also nurtures children's overall development, preparing them for a variety of future challenges and experiences.

Te Kura o Take Kārara

Incorporating Large Loose Parts in Outdoor Play

Preparing The Learning Environment

Chapter 3 – Checklist 1:

- Are you making use of PE equipment during play?
- Have you organised a range of large loose parts that can be used during outside play?
- Are the large loose parts set up in an attractive way that invites play?
- Have you ensured that there is ready access to sand and water play?
- Have you supplied real tools for sand and water play?
- Have you ensured there is a space for quiet outside play?
- Have you ensured you have a plan to reenergise the outside learning space?

Longworth Forest School

Promoting Learning to the School Community

Making Learning Visible

Key Pedagogical Principles: Student-Centred Learning, Constructivism, Reflective Practice

This chapter delves into the critical role of making learning visible and accessible to students through various forms of documentation. It explores how different methods of displaying learning, from visual displays to digital platforms like Seesaw and other narrative assessment platforms, can profoundly enhance students' understanding and involvement in their educational journey. The visibility of learning documentation is not just a method of record-keeping; it is a dynamic tool that can transform the educational experience.

Importance of Visible Learning Documentation:

Enhances Reflection and Self-Assessment: Visible documentation allows students to reflect on their learning journey, understand their progress, and identify areas for improvement. It fosters a culture of self-assessment and critical thinking.

Strengthens Connections Between Learning Experiences: By making learning visible, students can see the connections between different activities and how they relate to the broader curriculum. This understanding deepens their engagement with the material.

Promotes a Sense of Achievement and Motivation: Displaying students' work and progress instils a sense of pride and accomplishment. It motivates them to continue their efforts and take ownership of their learning.

Facilitates Teacher-Student Dialogue: Visible documentation opens up avenues for meaningful conversations between teachers and students about their work. It provides a basis for constructive feedback and collaborative planning for future learning activities.

Encourages Peer Learning and Collaboration: When students' work is visible to their peers, it promotes a learning community where students can learn from and be inspired by each other. It fosters a collaborative environment where students can share ideas and strategies.

As we delve into the topic of learning documentation, we once again employ our three-stage practice descriptor to guide our understanding and application of these concepts. This structured approach breaks down the process of making learning visible and accessible into distinct stages, each representing a progression in the effectiveness and depth of learning documentation. By exploring these stages, educators can gain insights into how to effectively document and display student learning, from basic methods to more advanced and interactive strategies. A self-assessment checklist is included at the end of the chapter, providing a practical tool for educators to reflect on their current documentation practices and explore ways to enhance the visibility of student learning in their classrooms.

Preparing The Learning Environment

Limited Visibility of Learning Documentation

At the minimal level, there is little to no learning documentation visible to students in the learning environment.

Characteristics: In this setting, students do not have access to displays or records of their learning activities. There is an absence of visual or digital documentation within the classroom.

St Patricks' School, Napier

Impact on Learning: Without visible documentation, students miss opportunities to reflect on their learning, share experiences, and connect activities to curriculum objectives.

Improvement Strategies: Introducing basic forms of documentation, such as photo displays or simple class journals, can start to bring learning activities into visibility.

Basic Learning Displays

At a developing stage, some aspects of learning are made visible through general displays and limited digital documentation.

Characteristics: Visual displays may include posters or scrapbooks showcasing play activities, with general links to learning outcomes like school values or social skills. Digital documentation, if present, is basic and may not fully capture the depth of learning.

Impact on Learning: These displays start to provide a sense of recognition

St Patricks' School, Napier

Promoting Learning to the School Community

and validation for students' activities. However, the connection to specific curriculum objectives may still be lacking.

Improvement Strategies: Enhancing displays to include more detailed links to curriculum objectives and expanding the use of digital platforms like Seesaw can provide a more comprehensive view of student learning.

Comprehensive and Interactive Learning Documentation

In a strong setting, learning documentation is extensive, interactive, and integrated into the classroom environment.

St Patricks' School, Napier

Characteristics: A mix of whole-class, group, and individual learning is documented and displayed. This includes narrative and visual assessments linked directly to curriculum objectives and core educational values. Digital media, along with their print versions, provide an interactive platform for students to engage with their learning stories.

Impact on Learning: This comprehensive approach to documentation allows students to actively engage with, reflect upon, and share their learning experiences. It fosters a deeper connection to the curriculum and promotes a sense of pride and accomplishment.

Improvement Strategies: Continually updating displays and digital documentation to reflect current learning themes and student interests can keep the documentation relevant and engaging. Involving students in the creation and curation of their learning stories can enhance their sense of ownership.

Chapter 4 - Checklist 1:

- Have you organised a space on the walls and /or in large scrapbooks for a display of whole class and group learning showing narrative and visual assessments?
- Have you shown in these visual displays, links to curriculum objectives, dispositions, school values, schema or school related learning?
- Have you ensured that individual learning stories are stored and displayed in individualised display books?
- Are the individualised display books readily available to your students to read independently and to share with friends and family?
- If you are using digital media for individual learning stories is there a print version available for students to access?

Parent Information and Communication Strategies

Key Pedagogical Principles: Family-Centred Practice, Holistic Education, Collaborative Learning

This chapter addresses the crucial aspect of communicating and engaging with parents about their children's learning experiences. It explores the effectiveness of various methods, including visual displays, newsletters, blogs, and digital media, in keeping parents informed and involved in the play-based learning process. Effective communication with parents is not just about providing information; it's about creating a partnership that enhances the educational experience for children.

Why Parent Education is Crucial?

Enhances Parental Understanding and Support: Keeping parents informed about the learning activities and the philosophy behind them helps build their understanding and appreciation of the play-based approach. This understanding fosters parental support both at home and in the school community.

Promotes Consistency Between Home and School: *Effective* communication ensures that the values and strategies of the play-based learning environment are mirrored at home, providing a consistent and supportive learning experience for the child.

Facilitates Parental Involvement and Engagement: When parents are well-informed, they are more likely to get involved in their child's education, whether through activities at home, participation in school events, or volunteering in the classroom.

Builds a Stronger School Community: Regular and transparent communication with parents helps build trust and a sense of community. It encourages a collaborative relationship where parents feel valued and welcomed as partners in their child's education.

Supports Individual Student Needs: By engaging with parents, teachers can gain insights into the child's strengths, challenges, and interests, which can be used to tailor educational experiences to better meet individual student needs.

Below we continue our exploration of key educational themes using the three-stage practice descriptor framework. This framework is designed to provide a clear and structured approach to understanding and enhancing parental engagement and communication in learning environments. Each stage represents a different level of effectiveness in engaging with parents, from initial efforts to comprehensive strategies. At the end of this chapter, you will find a self-assessment checklist. This tool is intended to help you evaluate your current practices in parental communication and identify areas for improvement, thereby fostering stronger connections between school and home.

Minimal Parental Communication

At the minimal level, there is scant communication between the teacher and parents regarding children's learning through play.

Characteristics: In this setting, there are few, if any, established channels for keeping parents informed about classroom activities and learning outcomes. There is a lack of effort to educate parents about the play-based learning approach.

Impact on Involvement: The absence of effective communication can lead to a disconnect between the school and home environments, hindering parents' understanding and involvement in their child's education.

Improvement Strategies: Initiating basic communication methods, such as regular newsletters or simple classroom blogs, can start to bridge the gap between the classroom and home.

St Patricks' School, Napier

Inconsistent Communication Efforts

At a developing stage, some efforts are made to communicate with parents, but these are inconsistent and may lack depth.

Characteristics: The teacher provides occasional updates through visual displays, newsletters, or online platforms. However, these communications might not consistently link to specific learning outcomes or the play-based learning philosophy.

Impact on Involvement: While these efforts provide a glimpse into the classroom activities, the sporadic nature of communication can leave parents partially informed and less engaged.

Promoting Learning to the School Community

Improvement Strategies: Regularizing and diversifying communication methods, such as consistent blog updates or using online narrative assessment tools, can enhance parental understanding and involvement.

Comprehensive and Regular Parent Engagement

In a strong setting, there is an ongoing and multifaceted approach to engaging parents in their children's learning journey.

Characteristics: Regular and informative parent evenings are organized, offering in-depth insights into the learning through play philosophy. Consistent communication is maintained through various means, including visual displays in the classroom, digital media updates, and interactive sessions where parents are invited to observe and participate in classroom activities.

Impact on Involvement: This comprehensive approach fosters a strong connection between the school and home environments. Parents are well-informed, engaged, and supportive of the play-based learning approach.

Improvement Strategies: Continuously seeking feedback from parents and adapting communication strategies to suit their needs can further strengthen this partnership. Encouraging parental involvement in classroom activities can also deepen their understanding and appreciation of the learning process.

Summary

Effective communication and engagement with both the school community and parents are fundamental to enriching the educational experience of children in a play-based learning environment. This chapter has highlighted the critical importance of making learning visible through documentation and establishing robust, diverse, and consistent communication pathways. These strategies are essential in keeping parents informed, involved, and supportive of their children's learning journey, thereby creating a more integrated and cohesive educational experience.

> Visible learning documentation serves not only as a reflective tool for students, enabling them to see and appreciate their progress and achievements, but also as a vital communication medium. It bridges the gap between the classroom and the wider community, showcasing the learning journey in a tangible and engaging manner. This approach recognises students as active participants in their education, empowering them to take ownership of their learning and to understand their developmental trajectory. It also allows educators to tailor their teaching strategies to meet the individual needs of each student, fostering a more personalised and effective learning environment.

Similarly, engaging parents through various communication strategies significantly strengthens the connection between school and home. It transforms parents from passive observers to active partners in their child's education. Regular and meaningful communication ensures that parents are not only informed but also feel valued and are able to contribute to their child's learning process. This partnership is crucial in creating a supportive and nurturing environment for children, both at school and at home.

Moreover, this comprehensive approach to documentation and communication extends beyond the immediate classroom. It fosters a collaborative and informed community, deeply involved in the educational journey. Parents and the wider school community become allies in the educational process, working together to support and enrich the learning experiences of children. This collaboration can lead to a more vibrant, dynamic, and inclusive educational culture, where the contributions and insights of every member are valued and utilised.

The practices of effective learning documentation and parental engagement are not just beneficial but essential in a play-based learning environment. They enhance the learning experience for students, foster a collaborative and informed community, and create a supportive network that surrounds and uplifts each child in their educational journey. By embracing these practices, educators can ensure a more holistic, engaging, and meaningful educational experience for all.

Chapter 4 – Checklist 2:

- Have you made time to hold a parent information evening?
- Have you arranged for ongoing and consistent communication with the parent community regarding the learning through play occurring in the classroom?
- Have you communicated to the parent community that they are welcome to visit the classroom to view the visual displays and /or learning stories?
- Have you set up a system whereby I can communicate with the parent community through digital media?

Conclusion: Shaping the Future through Play-Based Learning

As we conclude this handbook, it's essential to reflect on the journey that implementing play pedagogy can take. From understanding the nuances of choice and flexibility in learning environments to embracing the richness of small and large loose parts, and finally, to appreciating the significance of making learning visible and engaging the school community, each chapter has been a stepping stone towards creating a more holistic, dynamic, and inclusive educational experience.

> The foundation of this handbook lies in the belief that play is not just an activity; it's a vehicle for learning, exploration, and growth. The environments we create for our children greatly influence not just their academic development but their overall well-being. A play-based learning environment, infused with choice, flexibility, and diverse materials, caters to the unique needs of each child, fostering a sense of belonging, curiosity, and joy in learning.

Integrating Best Practices for Maximum Impact

The best practices outlined in this handbook are not isolated concepts but interconnected elements that create a cohesive and effective learning environment. Integrating these practices requires a thoughtful and intentional approach, one that considers the physical, emotional, and cognitive needs of children.

Fostering Choice and Flexibility: We've learned that choice and flexibility are not mere conveniences but essential components in fostering an engaging and responsive learning environment. Such an environment adapts to the evolving interests and needs of children, encouraging exploration, creativity, and independence.

The Role of Small and Large Loose Parts: The introduction of both small and large loose parts in learning spaces significantly enriches play experiences. These materials encourage children to think creatively, solve problems, and collaborate with their peers. They also play a crucial role in the physical, cognitive, and social-emotional development of children.

Making Learning Visible: Documenting and showcasing learning processes and outcomes not only enhances children's understanding of their learning journey but also fosters a deeper connection with their educational experiences. This visibility is a powerful tool that motivates and inspires both students and educators.

Engaging the School Community: Establishing robust and diverse communication pathways with parents and the wider school community strengthens the educational experience. By actively involving parents and caregivers, we create a supportive network that reinforces the values and practices of the play-based learning environment.

The Path Ahead: Challenges and Opportunities

While the journey towards creating and maintaining a play-based learning environment is rewarding, it's not without its challenges. Limited resources, space constraints, and varying levels of support can pose significant hurdles. However, these challenges also present opportunities for innovation, collaboration, and community engagement.

Educators are encouraged to be resourceful, to seek support from colleagues, parents, and the community, and to continuously adapt and evolve their practices to meet the changing needs of their students. The goal is not to create a perfect environment but to establish a space that is continually growing, changing, and improving.

Conclusion: Shaping the Future through Play-Based Learning

Inspiring Future Generations

As educators, our role extends beyond teaching academic skills. We are shaping the future by nurturing young minds that are curious, confident, and compassionate. By embracing the principles and practices outlined in this handbook, we are not just enhancing the educational experience of children; we are providing them with the tools, skills, and mindset to navigate the complexities of life.

Embracing Diversity in Play-Based Learning

Inclusivity and diversity are core principles of play-based learning. By designing learning environments that cater to a wide range of cultural backgrounds, abilities, and learning styles, we create a richer, more diverse experience for all children. This means incorporating materials, activities, and themes that reflect the varied experiences and identities of the children in our care. Embracing diversity in play encourages empathy, understanding, and respect among students, fostering a community where every child feels seen and valued.

The Power of Play in Emotional and Social Development

Play is not just about learning academic skills; it is also crucial for emotional and social development. Through play, children learn to navigate their emotions, develop empathy, build relationships, and resolve conflicts. In a play-based environment, educators have the unique opportunity to guide children through these social and emotional learning experiences, providing support and encouragement as they develop these essential life skills. By prioritising emotional and social development in our teaching, we prepare children to become compassionate, empathetic, and socially aware individuals.

Nurturing Creativity and Innovation

One of the most significant benefits of play-based learning is the nurturing of creativity and innovation. When children are given the freedom to explore, experiment, and express themselves, they develop a strong sense of creativity. This creative thinking is not just beneficial for artistic pursuits; it fosters a mindset that is critical for problem-solving and innovation in all areas of life. As educators, it's our role to provide an environment where creativity is not just allowed but actively encouraged and celebrated.

Conclusion: Shaping the Future through Play-Based Learning

The Role of Technology in Play-Based Learning

Incorporating technology into play-based learning can be both a challenge and an opportunity. While it's important to maintain a balance and ensure that technology does not dominate the learning experience, it can be a valuable tool in enhancing play and learning. Interactive digital resources, educational apps, and virtual collaborations can enrich the play experience, offering new ways for children to explore, create, and learn. However, it's crucial to use technology thoughtfully, ensuring it complements rather than replaces hands-on, physical play experiences.

Building a Sustainable Play Environment

Sustainability should be a key consideration in creating play-based learning environments. This involves using eco-friendly materials, promoting recycling and upcycling in play, and teaching children about environmental responsibility. By incorporating sustainability into play, we not only protect the environment but also instil in children a sense of responsibility and stewardship for the world around them.

Professional Development for Educators

For play-based learning to be truly effective, ongoing professional development for educators is essential. Training programmes, workshops, and collaborative learning opportunities allow educators to stay informed about the latest research, share best practices, and continuously improve their teaching methods. Investing in professional development ensures that educators are well-equipped to create dynamic, effective, and responsive learning environments.

Community and Parental Involvement

Finally, the involvement of the community and parents is crucial in enriching and supporting the play-based learning environment. Encouraging parents to participate in their child's learning, whether through classroom involvement, feedback, or support at home, strengthens the connection between the school and the home. Community partnerships can also provide additional resources, expertise, and opportunities for children to learn and engage with the world around them.

In conclusion, the journey towards a play-based learning environment is a continuous process of learning, adapting, and growing. It's about creating spaces that inspire, challenge, and support every child in their unique learning journey.

Conclusion: Shaping the Future through Play-Based Learning

About the Authors

Dr. Sarah Aiono

Dr. Sarah Aiono is an international speaker, coach, teacher, researcher, and one of Aotearoa New Zealand's leading experts in play pedagogy. With extensive experience as a classroom teacher, Sarah has a deep passion for supporting educators in implementing evidence-informed play practices that enhance student learning and wellbeing. As CEO and co-Director of Longworth Education, she leads a team dedicated to helping schools across New Zealand, Australia, Canada, and India integrate play into everyday classroom practices. Sarah is engaged in a variety of research projects, including co-lead investigator in exploring indigenous play practices in primary education. She supports various global organisations, including HundrED, the Global Recess Alliance, and Neurochild. Her contributions to education extend beyond the classroom, as she advocates for the importance of play in fostering innovation, creativity, and resilience in the business sector and wider society. Sarah's work has made her a respected voice in the global education community, where she continues to influence and inspire educators around the world.

Linda Cheer

Linda Cheer has held several teaching positions in her 40+ year career as an educator, including classroom teacher, team leader and Deputy Principal. In 2014, she established Longworth Forest School, a private facility where children aged 5-6 learned through hands-on, outdoor play and discovery in all weather conditions. Linda's passion for outdoor learning led her to create a natural environment at Longworth Forest that fostered key competencies and a deep connection with the natural world. The school's innovative approach was recognized in 2017 by the Finnish organization HundrED as one of a hundred global innovations in education. Linda brings a wealth of experience in implementing play-based learning from both a classroom and senior management perspective. As co-Director of Longworth Education, Linda now delivers workshops on play-based learning and supports teachers in bringing these practices to life in their classrooms. Her expertise and commitment have made her a sought-after speaker, including keynote engagements at Literacy Association Conferences.

www.ingramcontent.com/pod-product-compliance
Lightning Source LLC
Chambersburg PA
CBHW062043290426
44109CB00026B/2721